RICHMOND FREE LIBRARY
RICHMOND, VT. 05477
434 - 3036

A
Window
on
Vermont

D1600355

A Window on Vermont

Marguerite Hurrey Wolf

To Mary
with best wishes,
Maggie Wolf

The New England Press, Inc.
Shelburne, Vermont

© 1998 by Marguerite Hurrey Wolf

All rights reserved. No part of this book may be reproduced or transmitted in any form or by any means, electronic or mechanical, including photocopying, recording, or by any information storage and retrieval system, without permission in writing from the publisher, except by a reviewer, who may quote brief passages in a review.

Cover illustration by Livy Hitchcock
First edition
Printed in the United States of America

Library of Congress Catalog Card Number: 98-88001
ISBN 1-881535-32-0

For additional copies of this book or for a catalog of
our other New England titles, please write:

The New England Press
P.O. Box 575
Shelburne, VT 05482

or e-mail: nep@together.net

Visit us on the Web at www.nepress.com

Contents

Acknowledgments

Prime Time published several of my articles that are chapters in this book. They include:

    January
    February Patterns
    Spring at Last
    October's Bright Blue Weather
    What's Good about November?

The Burlington Free Press printed the following:

    Waiting for Spring
    Look Quick, It's Spring

And *The Elder's Advocate* gave their readers:

> Home Improvement
> What's Good about Getting Older?
> What's in a Name?

To these three organizations, my thanks for allowing these articles to be included in my book.

Introduction

We rarely choose where we will be born. Actually the baby never has a chance to choose, but occasionally the parents choose the place, if not the exact time. My mother told me about a few such arrangements. When my parents lived in Buenos Aires the English ladies, about to deliver, would go out on an English ship anchored in the harbor so that their babies would be born English, though not on English soil.

My sister was born in Buenos Aires but not on a ship. She was born in their apartment in the city, which made her an Argentine citizen. Her name was Frances, Francesca in Spanish, but her birth certificate read Francisco, the masculine ending. To my sister's surprise, when she turned twenty-one at Mt. Holyoke College she was notified that she was being called up for the Argentine army. She had to go to the Argentine embassy in New

York to prove in person that she was obviously female and establish her United States citizenship.

I was born in Montclair, New Jersey, and didn't lay eyes on Vermont until I was ten years old on my way to Maine. My mother, a lifelong teacher, thought it would be educational for us to go via Plymouth, Vermont, to see the homestead where Calvin Coolidge had recently taken the oath of office as president. We were cordially received by his father, Colonel Coolidge, who was sitting on the porch whittling walking sticks and selling them to dyed-in-the-wool Republicans like my father for $1.00 apiece. I wish I had that cane now.

Although I visited Vermont on several later occasions, it was not until George and I rented a friend's converted barn in Underhill for the month of August 1948 that we seriously hunted for a small, inexpensive rural spot as a summer haven to balance our winter New York City urban life.

Our brook and waterfall reached out and claimed us as though they had been waiting for us to see the light. Then our guardian Green Mountain angel offered George the deanship of the College of Medicine at UVM, and we became "year-round summer folks."

It wasn't until my aunt in Michigan, the family genealogist, read my first book in 1965 and indignantly assured me that I had several great-great-grandfathers whose Vermont farm is now the Brattleboro retreat that the stigma of being "from away"—even worse, "New

Yorkers"—was partially erased. After living here for fifty years, though not a native, I'm a Vermonter by choice.

Our only native Vermonter is grandson Morgan (17), son of our daughter Debbie and Steve Page. They live in Williston. Our daughter Patty, son-in-law Tage Strom, and their boys Patrick (22) and Peter (20) live in Montclair, New Jersey. Patrick is closing in on Vermonthood by virtue of graduating from UVM, and he is now working in Vermont. If he needs further accreditation, he can invoke his great-great-great-grandfathers.

And a Brook Runs Through It

Unlike the book *And a River Runs Through It*, this isn't about fishing, but it is about family relationships interwoven with the brook that runs through our land.

We first saw the brook with its waterfalls and pool in the summer of 1948. Most of the farms our friends or real estate agents had shown us as possible summer homes were too big and the houses too expensive. One day we stopped in Wayne Nealy's store in Jericho Center to buy a pair of jeans. Wayne sensed we were "from away," and, when we told him we were looking for a small farm with a brook, he told us about a place on the West Bolton road. He didn't tell us it was his father's farm that had stood empty for ten years. "Go down behind the barn to the river. It's a nice spot."

"Nice" was an understatement typical of Wayne. Debbie, 1½, and Patty, 4, pulled off their socks and sneakers and waded into the clear water. George and I were mesmerized by the series of waterfalls and potholes above the pool. No one wanted to leave, and we carried a kicking, loudly protesting Debbie back up to the car. We have belonged to these fifteen acres (more or less) for fifty years.

The next summer we painted the house, and I struggled to wallpaper a room that had four doors and four windows, each of a different size. George and a dentist friend put in a hot water heater, a septic tank, and plumbing of sorts. We installed a gas range, a toilet, and a kitchen sink, but the house was modernized only enough to enable us to spend the summers within the sound and sight of the brook. We swam in it. We washed ourselves and sometimes our clothes in it that first summer. We were especially proud of the original millstone wedged between two granite outcroppings. After all, it is named Mill Brook because its water powered several mills in the last century. Ours was a grist mill, but the only remaining evidence of the mill is the millstone and very faint wagon tracks leading down to the brook on the east boundary of our property. It was and is known as "Charley Nealy's fishing hole."

After four years, when George became dean of the College of Medicine at UVM (the University of Vermont) and we moved to South Burlington, we were able to spend all summer in Jericho. We couldn't live here in the winter because there was no foundation under the new (1890) part of the house and the plumbing was exposed to the elements.

Occasional fishermen tried their luck every spring, but they were no problem. One exception was a visit from Kermit Krantz, an obstetrician at the medical school. Kermit is an enthusiast. He makes a dramatic production out of everything, including fishing. He went down to the pool and within a few minutes came galloping up to the house waving a big brown trout. He borrowed a pail so that he could keep the fish alive and went back to the brook for more. Half an hour later I saw Kermit dragging up the path, uncharacteristically subdued. He put the pail on the doorstep and walked quietly back to his car. I went out to see if he was sick. "I filled the pail with water, put the fish in it, and left it on the bank. Right in front of my eyes that damned fish jumped out of the pail and back in the brook. I don't feel much like fishin' anymore but at least you saw it."

Our first summer in Jericho our girls were 2½ and 5, city children eager to learn about farm animals. Wayne Nealy still kept his cows on our land, and when a Jersey heifer was born he said the girls could keep her as a pet until we returned to the city. "Daisy," named for my mother, became very tame and considered herself one of the family. One day Fred Hale, business manager at the Mary Fletcher Hospital, came fishing and waded out knee deep in the pool. Daisy came galloping down the path, eager to make friends, and followed him into the water.

She kept following him deeper and deeper until the water was waist high on his waders. In desperation he climbed up on the rocks and fled to the house, where he breathlessly told me he had been chased by a Jersey bull. "You never can trust a Jersey bull!"

We had Fourth of July picnics at the pool in all weathers. Once it was so cold that we huddled over the fire. More often it was so hot that only our noses showed above the water.

For Debbie the brook has been the one constant in her life. Every summer from age 2½ until her marriage all or part of her summer was spent here. So it was quite natural that she wanted to be married at the pool. It was early October, and the foliage was at its peak. Debbie and Steve mowed the grass—it was going to be idyllic. But it rained the day of the wedding. It had been raining for two days before that. The path was a running brook. Undeterred, they insisted on being married down there, so we outfitted everybody with boots, umbrellas, and rain coats and huddled under a quickly erected tent.

Debbie's dog, an enthusiastic golden retriever who loved to dash into the brook and then come out and shake all over everyone, had been given half of a tranquilizer pill to calm him down. It didn't seem to take effect, so Steve gave him the other half of the pill. As "best dog" he was part of the wedding party, but he stole the show. His gait became unsteady. He had trouble focusing his eyes, a perfect imitation of a drunk. During the ceremony he solemnly looked up at Debbie when she spoke, then struggled to focus on Willy Cochran who, as justice of the peace, was performing the ceremony.

Three days of rain had turned the waterfall into a raging Niagara. The spoken words and the trumpet solo played by Jim Landon were nearly drowned out by the roar of the brook.

It was one of the happy times at the brook, but there have been scary ones as well. We assumed that every ten-year-old could swim, but when Donald Riker slipped off the inner tube he was playing with, he sank right down to the bottom under the waterfall. George dove in and had to pull him up to the surface. Fortunately he hadn't inhaled any water, but he was a pale and subdued little boy.

And then there was the sad spring when George died, at home the way he wanted it, just fading away. He had asked to be cremated and said he didn't care what we did with the ashes. "Throw them in the brook and they'll end up in Lake Champlain." Somehow that didn't seem enough. With Patty and Debbie and the three grandsons, we took the ashes down to the brook and buried them next to the big boulder known as the "dressing rock." In all our years here, even when the snow melt makes the pool surge up over the grassy bank, water has never reached that rock. That summer there were unusually heavy rains, and the brown turbulent water swirled up around the boulder. I hesitated to tell the girls. When I phoned Patty I heard funny sounds. I was afraid she was crying. But she was laughing. "Pop said we should throw the ashes in the brook." But the brook came up and claimed them. Death was a part of his life, and a brook ran through it.

Window on Wildness

No matter where you live in Vermont, you are always within reach of the restorative presence of wildness. My house is within a stone's throw of Vermont's largest city—if you have a phenomenally strong arm—but I live in the country with no other house in sight, on a small stream called Mill Brook because it supported several mills. The one on our property was a grist mill dating from 1820. All that remains of the mill is the millstone wedged between rocky outcroppings. It would be as hard to pry me loose from these fifteen acres, more or less, as it would be to extricate that millstone from the clutch of granite ledge.

We built the new house facing the brook, on a wooded hillside several hundred feet above the pool, so that the sound and sight of the waterfall is always with us. Mesmerizing as this is, I can't spend all day watching the pool, but while I am eating breakfast or happen to glance out the window I occasionally have a front row seat at a wildlife drama. I wish I were included more often. I hate to think of the interesting visitors that I have missed, and many of my regulars are nocturnal. The holes all over my lawn tell me that skunks have been digging for grubs. Deer and snowshoe hares leave their footprints in the snow all around the house, and raccoons check out the birdfeeders nightly. I do see the raccoons if I turn on the outside light. They glance up nonchalantly but unafraid until I open a window. Then they waddle awkwardly down into the woods, where they live in a rocky cave.

My rarest nocturnal visitor was a flying squirrel, the only one I've seen here. It was almost dark when I noticed reddish-orange eyes shining in a nearby tree. A very large squirrel with unusually big eyes suddenly stretched out in a heroic leap, spread his "wings," the folded layer of loose skin along each side of his body, and sailed at least fifteen feet to another tree.

Dawn or dusk is the most likely time for my shy neighbors to be abroad. One summer evening I saw a streak of brown through the underbrush. A slender, silky weasel undulated up over a big boulder, stretched up on his hind legs to get a good look at me with his shoe button eyes, and then vanished. We saw him again in winter, snow white with a black tip on his tail, almost completely camouflaged against the snow. A weasel is not an animal most people admire. He is sly, clever,

12

and a vicious adversary. But whatever you may think of a weasel's personality, remember that for four months of the year he becomes an ermine, symbol of royalty and grandeur.

I was lucky enough to see a bobcat once, but only because he announced his presence with a wild cry meant to intimidate me. It did. I flicked on the light and saw him crouched on a low branch of a tree, twice the size of a house cat, with a stub of a black-tipped tail and slightly tufted ears. His eyes flashed and he snarled at me before he leapt to the ground and melted into the woods.

Only occasionally do I see a deer from my window. One winter morning at breakfast I noticed that the pool was almost entirely frozen over, with just a crescent of black open water below the waterfall. A young doe was standing on the ice, front legs spread apart as she leaned down to drink from the open water. She stepped forward and crashed through the fragile ice into the pool. I watched helplessly as she thrashed about, desperately trying to get a firm hold on the ice with her forelegs. I found myself straining and willing her to try harder again and again.

Finally with a monumental heave she lunged up onto the ice, scrambled to her feet, shook off the icy water, and slowly made her way up into the woods on the opposite side of the pool. I sighed with relief, turned back to my breakfast, and then glanced up to see something move on the ice. A coyote, tail drooping and head lowered, was sniffing at the spot where the doe had been. He had obviously caught the scent of the young doe and, nose to the ice, followed the same path she had taken into the woods. In five minutes this silent drama had taken me from despair to elation to fear and apprehension. Who says that life in the country is uneventful?

At dinner one evening a movement outside caught my eye, and I looked out straight into the huge, horse-like face of a female moose, not ten feet away, staring at me in equal surprise. A moose, right at the edge of my deck! I had seen moose standing knee deep in a swamp both in Maine and in the Northeast Kingdom, but a moose on land and very close is amazingly large—six feet at the shoulder and weighing more than six hundred pounds. The legs are very slender and long, and the enormous head, with its overhanging snout and pendant bell on the throat, seems all out of proportion to its body.

Albinism occurs now and then in wildlife. So does melanism, the black opposite of the pigmentless albino. One early spring I saw a black woodchuck near the house, but when I told my husband about it he scoffed and said it probably was a black house cat or a fisher. Now a woodchuck doesn't look like either of those, and I was insulted enough to bait the Hav-a-hart trap with some tasty greens. Eureka! The next morning the black woodchuck was in the trap, and I gloated shamelessly. I wanted to show it off but no interested neighbors were at home, so we had to release it way up the road well beyond the houses. No one wants a surplus woodchuck, even if it is black.

I have seen a black bear, but not from my window. It was a small cub at the side of the road, but I didn't get out of the car, believing that the sow was nearby and might not welcome my interference. If I kept bees, as some of my neighbors do, I would be more likely to be visited by bears—a doubtful honor, in my opinion.

And there was the time we were kept under house arrest by a militant female grouse, which attacked us every time we opened the door. She must have had a nest nearby, but we never found it. I admired her courage, but it prevented me from transplanting the annuals for a week.

Now that the catamount has returned to Vermont, do you think there's a chance that I may look up from my dinner into the green-gold eyes of that symbol of Vermont wildlife? I'll let you know.

January

It's that time of year again, when, like the Roman god *Janus,* we find ourselves looking back over the old year and forward to the new. It was easy for him because he had two faces, one in front and one behind, which made him a natural for his job as Gatekeeper of Heaven.

I'm no gatekeeper. But as I pack away the Christmas tree ornaments, take a last look at the Christmas cards, and ferret out the pine needles buried in the depths of my old shag rug, I am still surrounded by the debris of Christmas, yet eager to put it away and explore the possibilities of the new year.

By the time I have disentangled the last strands of tinsel from my sweater and taken down the greens, the room looks suddenly bare, neat but empty. But nature abhors a vacuum. The first seed catalogues arrive in the mailbox to brighten up the coffee table and lull me into my annual midwinter night's dream.

What is so glorious as that array of scarlet, smooth, perfectly round tomatoes, golden ears of corn, purple satin eggplants, and pole beans that emulate Jack's beanstalk and could only be picked by Michael Jordan? It is easy to forget that after transplantation my tomatoes sat and sulked for two weeks before deciding to put out new leaves, or that my eggplants lived up to their name by only reaching the size of pullet's eggs before the first frost. You may have outgrown your childhood belief in the Easter Bunny and Santa Claus, but deep in the heart of every gardener worth his superphosphate is the abiding faith that THIS year his beans will snap, his corn will repel the raccoons, and his potatoes will emerge into the light of day round and scab free.

And do you know what? Faith can move mountains. Well, not mountains, perhaps, but it will move the multitude of rocks that Mother Earth propels to the surface each spring. They are Vermont's most predictable crop. This fantasy includes deep rich soil just moist enough by the last week in May, a dearth of black flies in June, and a total absence of potato bugs and cucumber beetles in July, thanks to careful planting of garlic, nasturtiums, marigolds, and such pest repellents as basil, thyme, and catnip. And, if you have a cat-loving friend, she'll bless you for giving her cats some intoxicating days.

Now back to the reality of January, a month lacking in holidays except for the remembrance of Martin Luther King. There may be power outages, deep snow, even deeper cold, and cars off the road. My grandmother had a cross-stitched motto that read, "Let me live in a house by the side of the road and be a friend to man." I do live in a house by the side of a dirt road, which amuses itself in January by luring unsuspecting motorists into its ditches. There is no other house for half a mile east or a quarter of a mile west of mine, so guess whose house beckons as a friend to man, woman, or teenager during the icy months? When I hear the wheels spinning I know there will soon be a knock on the door and a request to use the phone. I don't see myself as a St. Bernard dog with a keg of brandy around my neck, but I can at least phone to my neighbor, Cary Todriff, who earns part of his living and a lot of good will by pulling out ditched cars for a moderate fee. Cary is one of those rare people who is cheerful at four o'clock in the morning when it is twenty below. In fact, he has probably been up awhile plowing out the driveways of the families on my back road. Now *he* is a friend to man, better than a St. Bernard in our mechanized world.

January gives you respect for the power of nature. When it is so cold that your boots squeak and the air is full of minute ice crystals, it helps to remember that apple trees need the rest period of cold to produce good fruit. It is a thaw that harms apple trees. Robert Frost wrote: "No orchard's the worse for the wintriest storms. But one thing about it, it mustn't get warm." Perhaps we too need a rest period, a time to look back at whatever was good and bad in the old year and forward to what we can hope to achieve in the new. To appreciate warmth you need to come in out of the cold and be greeted by the smell of something savory on the stove and the face of someone loved.

It was dark by 4:30 in December, but now each day the sun sets a little later, and for a brief period the setting sun ignites the snow-covered mountains with a rosy glow—blue shadows stretch out across the fields. Winter won't be over for nearly three more months, but the midwinter night's dream will come true.

Think Spring

It's never too early to start dreaming of spring. Well, maybe not in January. Certainly not during the great ice storm of '98, when trees were snapping, branches breaking, and all you were dreaming of was the return of "the electric" for heat and light.

But today is Groundhog Day, February 2. The sun is out and the chuck saw his shadow this morning. So you can guarantee that we'll have six more weeks of winter. That's not news in Vermont. No matter what the ground- hog saw when he crawled out of bed, you know we'll have six more weeks of winter, at least. That would only take us to the Ides of March, and some of our greatest snowfalls have been in March.

Forget Groundhog Day or Candlemas. That myth started in England, where they have flowers in March, for heaven's sake, while we're still sanding, shoveling, and sniffling.

What I get the urge to do from February 2 on is to hunt for signs of spring. The first and most rewarding in terms of my outlook on life is the lengthening of days. It is still light at 5:15! It is wonderful to come home from an afternoon meeting bathed in the afterglow of the sunset. The snow on Mt. Mansfield is the delicate pink of the inside of a seashell, and the western sky over the Adirondacks is an assortment of citrus colors, lime green, lemon yellow, and tangerine. It's not only the plants that thrive under light.

I need that big Gro-Light in the sky to bolster my winter-weary spirits. And with the return of that light, somewhere down under the snowdrifts new warmth must be filtering through to trigger renewed growth.

Off in the woods a flicker is hammering imperatively, announcing his territorial claims. Two grey squirrels are chasing wildly around and up and down a maple tree in a frenetic courtship. Maybe you don't think of a squirrel as a harbinger of spring, but they are most amorous as Valentine's Day approaches.

On a warm day the sound of icicles dripping from the eaves is a premonition, however fleeting, and my brook is loudly protesting under its icy bondage.

The mail brings catalogs touting new clothes in pastel colors. Even L. L. Bean features fishing equipment rather than snowshoes.

There is talk of Town Meeting in the village store although the date is a month away. And up and down the road, sap buckets are sprouting on the maple trees, in spite of the warnings that some maples may have been so severely damaged by the ice storm that they shouldn't be tapped this year. Not tap the maples? Heresy in Vermont.

Don't hang up your shovel yet, but it is fun to dream about the day when you can fling open the windows, walk out to the mailbox without a coat, and hang sheets on the line to snap and billow in the wind.

You'll need your boots for another two months, for snow and then mud. Am I the only one who welcomes mud season? It too is a sure sign of spring. You may slip on it, get stuck in it, and bemoan its adhesive qualities to dogs, boots, and small boys, but it tells you that the frost is coming out of the ground.

One morning an optimistic chickadee changes his staccato notes to the more melodic "spring soon." Any day now a well concealed ruffed grouse ("patridge" in these parts) will take his stand on some log and thump his slowly accelerated drumming to announce his availability.

On a moonlit night you may see a skunk ambling along on the shrinking snow. I doubt if the ground is soft enough for him to dig up grubs. But in another month the lawn will be pocked with his excavations.

Our resident raccoon is spending less time in his den and more looking for a mate. I can hear him at night on the porch, checking out the bird feeder. When I turn on the porch light he stares at me complacently until I open the window and shout at him. He gives me one last look and then waddles down the hillside towards his den. The next night he may bring his mate and that too is a sign of spring, because in winter, when he occasionally ventures out of the garden, he is always alone. It will turn cold again, and he and I will both crawl back in bed, where I'll dream of snowdrops, pussy willows, and the sweet earthy fragrance of spring.

February Patterns

The month of February is mercifully short and full of holidays—Valentine's Day, Lincoln's and Washington's birthdays, and, as a resident of Jericho, I would add Snowflake Bentley's birthday on February 9.

Surely you've heard about our most famous citizen, who studied and photographed snowflakes just half a mile up the road from my house. He was a farm boy taught at home by his mother, a former schoolteacher. She gave him a microscope, and, through trial and error, he learned to carefully mount a flake on black velvet and photograph it in a cold shed. It was delicate and tedious work with his three-foot bellows camera, but it became his consuming passion from 1885 till his death in 1931. During that time he photographed 5,831 different forms of ice crystals.

He was considered odd by his Jericho neighbors because he was more interested in a raindrop than in farming. He did his own sap boiling and was a skillful hay loader in spite of his slight build, but he was less interested in milking than in comparing snowflakes. He never found two alike. He was largely ignored in his home town. In 1924 he received the first research grant ever awarded by the American Meteorological Society, but when he offered to show his slides for free on a summer evening in Jericho, only six people showed up.

It was not until 1931, shortly before his death, that his book *Snow Crystals* was published. Now Tiffany uses his photographs for their jewelry designs, and the Air Force relies upon his findings for the study of atmospheric conditions.

And then comes a very ancient holiday. St. Valentine, the Roman martyr priest whose feast is February 14, became the patron of love because the day coincided with the festival of *Lupercalia*. The symbols of this holiday have been hearts (often shot through by an arrow), lovebirds, and flowers. The Valentines we made as children were made with red paper hearts, lace doilies, cupids, and bluebirds. We pasted them together, fastening the lace doilies on top of the hearts with little folded paper hinges. It was delicate work when you were ten years old but worth it on the day you took them to school and slid them into the slot of the red crepe paper-covered cracker box on the teacher's desk. There was such excitement when they were distributed and you tried to figure out whom "guess who" was.

But February has other patterns, some of them right outside my window. On the snow-covered path to the brook there is a chain of deer prints where it walked down to drink from the only unfrozen spot in the pond under the waterfall. And under the bird feeder is a lacy network of bird prints making five-pointed designs rather than the six-pointed pattern of every snowflake.

Today I saw another set of patterns—children were making angels in the snow just the way we did sixty years ago. They would flop down on their backs, spread their arms, and wave them up and down to shape angel wings. Once, when we lived in New York City in the 1940s, there was an unusually heavy snowstorm. The streets were snow-covered, silent, and devoid of traffic. It was such a rare opportunity in the city that three or four of us ran out into the street and made angels the way we had as children.

I noticed another February pattern a few years ago. I was flying back to Burlington. The lady in the seat next to me commented on the large, dark circles on the snowy fields below. She thought they were beautiful and wondered what they could be. Her admiration dimmed when I told her these patterns were made by farmers' manure spreaders circling the fields, unloading their enriching by-product. Other snow designs are visible from the ground. Long ribbons of ski tracks are embroidered with dots made by the ski poles and inter-twine with the wide, swooping circles of snowmobile tracks.

But the most beautiful patterns are the natural snow sculptures, where the wind has piled up waves of snow into crests that arc over blue shadows and seem about to collapse into the sea of snow. The lacy patterns of bare branches against a bluet-colored sky have individual personalities—there are the stately upswept arms of the elms, the golden cast on the weeping willows, and the tiny knobs of buds on the poplar trees. These waxy buds won't open for two months, but they contain the pattern of new life, fully formed and tightly encapsulated, waiting for light and warmth to trigger their unfolding.

The worst rigors of winter seem to be behind us. That may not be true. March can be a stormy month. But with the lengthening days the rest is downhill—skidding and slipping, perhaps, but headed in the direction of spring.

Home Improvement?

Have you ever watched "Home Improvement" on TV? When Tim suggests something totally outrageous, Al quietly replies, "I don't think so, Tim," with a significant look at the audience. I'm with Al.

There are some "improvements" at home and in the market place that I would put in the If-it-ain't-broke-don't-fix-it category.

When I wash my hands in a rest room I don't enjoy wringing them frantically in front of the hand dryer blower. And when it goes off I still have to wipe my hands on something—anything! The old paper towels weren't what you could call downy, but at least they absorbed most of the moisture. And while we're still in the rest room, don't you miss the hook on the inside of the door of the toilet booth where you could hang your handbag?

28

I heard they were removed because some nefarious types reached over the closed doors and purloined some purses. Now you can set your handbag on the floor or balance it on the back of the toilet, hoping it won't fall in when you rise from the seat.

There are various areas in which I am still mired in the dark ages. Can you believe I still have a dial phone? I am perfectly happy with it until I call some business and they begin a litany of numbers for me to press to reach the different departments. After about the sixth I get so bored that I hang up. But worse is, "Our lines are all busy. We will connect you as soon as there is an open line." And while you stay on the phone hoping for the sound of a live voice on comes another recorded message.

Many of my friends have answering machines. Why do they always say, "We can't come to the phone right now"? Of course they can't. They aren't there. Everyone knows it, but they don't dare say, "I'm not home." Whom are they kidding?

Now let's talk about some improvements on our daily round of errands. I'm not happy in an ATM booth. Somehow I can't rid myself of the entertaining fantasy of a tiny teller running around in there, checking my account balance and counting out the bills. Can't you hear his little feet? I'd rather go inside the bank and talk to a live teller, even though she will probably call me by my first name despite our not having met before.

Next stop, drug store. Am I the only adult who cannot open child-proof pill bottles? My grandson opened one for me when he was five years old, but when I press and turn, the top hangs on for dear life, sending me the message that I'm stupid. Eventually I have to pry it off.

Next stop, supermarket. They have "improved" packaged meats so much that along with the skin and bones they have removed the flavor. Remember when chicken tasted like chicken? When I was a child the chicken was cut up in front of you at the butcher store and a piece of chuck was ground before your eyes. You saw how much fat and gristle went in. You didn't have to read the percentage on the package.

And processed cheese! What is the process, taste removal? I prefer cheese made from whole milk rather than oil and water.

Prepared foods are convenient for women who don't get home until twenty minutes before suppertime. But they are expensive. I'm told time is money, and I'm glad I have time now and then to let a pot roast simmer for nearly four hours.

I don't go to the movies often, but when I do I am overwhelmed by the size of the screen. Is that what "in your face" means? Sweat is to be expected on an athlete but is hardly romantic in a love scene. Don't they know that black lace is sexier than nudity? Leave something to the imagination.

I have a friend who has an "improved" car. It talks. The baritone voice says, "Please fasten your seat belt" and thanks you when you do. He reminds you to get gas and windshield washer fluid. I don't want my car to talk to me. I want to talk to it, to praise it when it maneuvers out of a snow bank and to cuss it out when it gets lost in a parking lot.

Do I need a car to tell me when to turn the lights off or to remove the keys from the ignition? I don't think so, Tim.

Waiting for Spring

Two years ago we had the best skiing in years. Records were broken for the amount of snow and the number of days below zero. And the nights! It was thirty-nine below at my house one night, the coldest in the fifty years we've been here. It was below zero so many nights in January that it was beginning to seem normal. The house didn't agree and protested loudly with booming sounds in the beams. They call that nail popping, but it doesn't sound like the sound a nail would make if it did pop. When I looked at my electric meter that kilowatt hour recorder was whirling around like a pinwheel.

I thanked God and the Vermont Electric Cooperative that there were no outages. When you live in the country dependent on your own well, a power outage means not only no light, TV, typewriter, part of your heat, and stove, but also no *water* and the additional risk of your water line freezing.

I'm grateful also to Cary Todriff for keeping my driveway plowed, even though he had to use a bucket loader once after the piles were higher than six feet.

Yes, it was beautiful, and I know that three feet of snow is good insulation for the house and water line. But that was two years ago and now it is March and the charm of winter is wearing pretty thin. I do not yearn for another blizzard. I'm yearning for green and more than just on St. Patrick's Day. No wonder green is his color. In Ireland right now daffodils are in bloom and the grass is the color ours won't achieve until May.

Waiting is never easy. Remember how hard it was to wait for Christmas when you were small? And when you woke at the first light of dawn it was almost unbearable agony to wait for the rest of the family to finally get up and come downstairs.

Fast food emporiums were successful because it was always so hard for small children to wait for the food to be served in restaurants. Even at twenty, when my hollow-legged grandson comes for a family dinner, he says, "Grandma, would you PLEASE pick up your fork. Mom says I can't eat until you start."

When we took car trips with our children we were hardly out of the driveway before Debbie started her litany of "Are we almost there yet?"

33

It is not Christmas or dinner that I'm waiting for these days. It is spring. Along about the middle of March I can't wait for my favorite season. I applaud every bucket or plastic bag I see on a maple tree. I delight in the music of dripping icicles. Even the deep mud ruts on my road sucking at my tires remind me that if mud season comes can spring be far behind? The increased warmth of the sun and the lengthening days wake my hibernating spirits. This year we've been teased by alternating thaws and sudden drops in temperature. Just when the snow receded enough to expose a small patch of garden we had a blizzard that dumped more than a foot of snow, shoving us back into the deep freeze. Winter Wonderland? Been there. Had that. I want to see a robin winning a tug of war with a worm on my lawn. I want to hear redwings creaking in the cat tails. I want to wash and put away woolen socks and mittens. I'm so old fashioned that I want to hang my laundry on the clothesline and let the March wind billow and snap the sheets.

California asparagus and strawberries show up in the store. I welcome them as a sign of spring, but I'm going to wait two months for my own amethyst tips of asparagus to poke through the damp earth in my garden. It's disloyal to them to cater to those tourists "from away."

Another sign of spring, but not the most photogenic, is the flotsam and jetsam that surfaces when the snow recedes—gravel, beer cans, a soggy mitten, and part of a muffler that were mercifully concealed for four months. But looking for more attractive signs I'm tempted to poke down through the shrinking granular snow on the flowerbeds to see if the daffodils have started up. They may have because on the lawn of the library in Essex Junction I thought I saw something green. I knelt down and stared hungrily at the tiny green spikes. A deep voice behind me inquired, "Have you lost something?" "No, I've found something—crocus leaves!" The startled expression on his face turned into a grin. "You mean there WILL be a spring again this year?"

Yes, there will, but waiting is never easy. I need to go out to meet it. I will hunt for a few pussy willows and pat the swelling buds on the lilacs. I will go down to the pasture spring, pull away the sodden leaves, and think about Robert Frost. You come too!

In Praise of Common Things

Odes have been written to nightingales and larks, but have you ever read a sonnet extolling the magnificent plumage of a blue jay? A dandelion is a sunburst of golden petals, yet we do our best to root it out of our lawns. There is nothing more miraculous than the intricate pattern of a snowflake, each six-sided bit of lacy design different from every other one in the universe, but how often do we stop shoveling the walk to study and admire its delicate beauty?

They are too common. Millions of snowflakes are falling right now outside my window. In another month my field will be starred with a thousand dandelions, and I will be shooing the raucous blue jays away from my bird feeder. It's time to stop and admire what Wordsworth called "the unassuming commonplace of nature" around us every day. When the maple trees start to put out the tiny blossoms that precede their leaves, look at the unique arrangement of minute rosy petals.

We turn up our noses at corned beef and cabbage except on St. Patrick's Day, but it is more satisfying and has more flavor than pheasant under glass any old day. What can compare to the comforting memory of milk toast when you were sick in bed as a child or a bowl of chicken soup when a virus has taken the joy out of life?

Elysian fields couldn't compare with our meadow when a baby lamb was leaping in stiff-legged circles around its mother. I watched an ant carrying what looked like a tiny egg across the sidewalk, and I was awed by his dedication to the job at hand. No matter what small object I put in his path—a twig, a pebble, a blade of grass—he crawled over it or around it and continued in his original direction.

The roses don't need us to stop and smell them. They are acclaimed in verse, painted, sold for exorbitant prices, and even hybridized so competitively that there is no fragrance to smell if you do stop. It would be more rewarding to stop and smell the tiny purple violets almost hidden in the grass. Or watch a robin construct a sloppy but efficient nest out of mud, carried little by little in its beak into the branches of the chosen tree. Listen to a hermit thrush at sundown and you'll think that James Galway is hidden in the woods.

Elizabeth Barrett Browning wrote, "Earth's crammed with heaven, and every common bush afire with God."

Look Quick, It's Spring

You'd better keep your eyes open. If you blink you might miss spring altogether. It's our shortest and most elusive season. While you are resting on your shovel after digging out from under all the snow, spring creeps up behind you and tosses out a handful of gold.

> Nature's first green is gold
> Her hardest hue to hold.
> So dawn goes down to day
> Nothing gold can stay.

Robert Frost was right. Long before tiny leaves have appeared on the willow trees, there is a golden mist trapped in the branches. You can see this change in March some years, one of the first signs of spring. And a scattering of yellow crocuses on the lawn are my first flowers since the indomitable snowdrops shouldered their way up through the snow in response to the increasing light.

On the north side of my barn there is still a ridge of granular snow, but on the south side, where the sun has warmed the earth, one or two dandelions sparkle in the awakening grass. Even the pussy willow's velvet buds now have a dusting of yellow pollen.

Cowslips lure you into their watery habitat to pick them, but it is a risky enterprise. When Debbie was about two, she followed their siren call and snatched two small fistfuls of the golden globes. But when she tried to retrace her steps her small red rubber boots were stuck fast in the dark ooze. She had to step out of the boots, plunging her pink toes into the icy water. She held on to the cowslips, though! You have to grasp spring firmly or it will slip through your fingers.

On a trip to Maine one late April we marveled at the forsythia that was spilling over every stone wall in golden fountains. We don't have that much forsythia in Jericho, and my one bush only blossoms on the branches that have been covered with snow. Our heavy snow has delayed it this year, but there should be a lot of blooms because the bush completely disappeared under the huge piles of snow shoved over it by Cary Todriff's snowplow.

Spring is tentative in April. You can see her peeking shyly out of the woods in the delicate puffs of shadbush blossoms. But the next day she slips back deeper in the forest for protection from the pelting rain. April is full of promises, broken one day and fulfilled the next.

> Oh, to be in England
> Now that April's here.

Browning had a good idea, because April in Vermont doesn't mean that spring has arrived. But the gardener yearns for signs of spring. If the ground would only dry out you could put in some onion sets and winter tolerant seeds like lettuce, radishes, and spinach. I had a small salad garden in a spot that dried out long before the main garden, and I often planted it in mid-April. Of course germination is slower in cold ground, but it is so exciting to see something green poking through the earth. Radishes germinate quickly, so I always plant some in the rows of the later vegetables.

There are still patches of snow on my main garden. It won't be dry enough to rototill until mid-May, but I can pull away the old dried asparagus foliage and pull up any dandelions and other weeds that have sprouted there. The advantage of pulling dandelions when the earth is wet is that the whole long root comes up easily. And of course I can cut off the tender young leaves for my first spring tonic, a salad of store lettuce enlivened by dandelion and violet leaves. They're full of iron, and violet leaves have more vitamin C than an orange.

41

Shakespeare was never in Vermont, poor man, but when he wrote about "the uncertain glory of an April day," he might have been talking about our unpredictable weather. April is like a thirteen-year-old girl. You never know when she comes home from school whether she is going to act like a twenty-three-year-old or a three-year-old. But fortunately neither mood lasts long.

The showers of April are followed by clear blue skies. The sun has real warmth, and growth has started. At the end of maple season the maple trees are covered with tiny red blossoms. The delicate pink and white flowers of the shadbush open, and even the flower beds show signs of life. March's snowdrops are going to seed, but the slender green spears of daffodils are pushing up through the moist earth. A patch of blue scillas reflects the deep blue April sky. "April's in the west wind and daffodils," Masefield wrote, but he too lived in England, where the west wind was tempered by the Gulf Stream. Our daffodils won't blossom until May, but they are my most dependable spring flowers, largely because the voles and chipmunks are wise enough to know that the bulbs are poisonous and leave them alone.

The birds are back. Robins are listening for worms on the lawn and carrying dabs of mud to build their sloppy nests. The chickadees have changed their tune, and the redwing blackbirds are creaking in the wetlands.

If Easter comes in mid-month my lawn is spangled with crocuses in Easter colors—golden yellow, lavender, deep purple, and striped violet and white. Once again I will hide Easter eggs for my grandsons. The two who will be here this year are sixteen and twenty-one, but they won't let go of the tradition. I think I am humoring them. They think they are indulging me. Isn't that what the grandson-grandmother relationship is all about?

Secret Places

I have four grandcats. Asics and Ito enjoy the services of Debbie, Steve, and Morgan in Williston. Jaguar and Fizz are the benign despots who rule the household of Tage, Patty, Patrick, and Peter in Upper Montclair, New Jersey.

We always had cats when we lived in South Burlington during the school year and in Jericho in the summer. With one or two exceptions they were barn cats who spent the night with a horse, two pigs, and two sheep.

Now, with a small house and no farm animals, I really don't want to be owned by a cat. I have enough trouble avoiding falls without a cat weaving back and forth in front of my toes. Even when I was much younger I sometimes tripped over one of our cats. There was vocal indignation on both sides but no serious injuries. Now, I'm not so sure.

But I'm very familiar with cat idiosyncrasies. Every cat we ever had would jump into an empty carton or a reclining grocery bag. I have a basket that I use to transport odds and ends. When I take anything to Debbie's house, Asics, the mother cat, can hardly wait till I empty the basket. She immediately jumps into it, wrapping her tail around her and purring her approval. We smile indulgently, but don't we share some atavistic urge to curl up in some hiding place? Our ancestors lived in caves for more centuries than we have lived in houses.

On rainy days when I was small, I would turn over my father's big arm chair, throw a steamer blanket over it, and revel in my secret den. When I was eleven I had a tree house that a neighbor boy and I built in our big sweet cherry tree. It was at least eight feet off the ground, and we had a rope ladder that we could pull up after us, feeling safe from imagined enemies below. Our only real visitors were an occasional friendly dog or one of our curious parents, but we felt inviolable.

I loved the book *The Secret Garden,* and in Montclair, on Irwin Park Road, there was a real secret garden, fenced in but with a latched gate you could open. It was a lovely woodsy spot enclosed with tall hedges so that the interior wasn't visible from the street. We were told that it was a memorial to someone, but the owner made it available to anyone who wanted a peaceful moment in this sylvan space.

When we had an unusually heavy snowfall the immediate urge was to build a fort or, better still, an igloo. It was quite a trick to cut blocks for the igloo and even harder to place them in a diminishing circle without total collapse. But what ecstasy it was to crawl into the dim blue-white interior and bask in icy privacy.

We no longer need a cave to escape from saber-toothed tigers or a yurt to shield us from Siberian wintry blasts. I don't turn armchairs over and cover them with blankets anymore, and I haven't been in a tree house for years, but I can remember the comforting sense of seclusion from the adult world.

When Morgan was in grade school he barricaded himself in his room behind a door plastered with dire warnings—"Do NOT enter," "This means YOU," "Danger." I would never have trespassed on his privacy. Now he has a basement computer room where he holes up to compose electronic music and communicate with distant computer friends. I hesitate before I knock on this door.

I'm sorry for latchkey children. Home alone can be scary. We all need the reassurance that help and companionship are nearby if needed, but the freedom to pull in the latchstring and dream in a secret place should be the right of every child.

As Ye Sow

Look before ere you leap
For as you sow, you are likely to reap.

Samuel Butler wrote that 300 years ago. It's still true. How about those six zucchini seeds you planted that produced 180 squashes? We should have looked before we leapt into pine tree planting. Thirty-eight years ago we planted 8,000 white pine seedlings following the best advice of the time. Our rocky pastures were no longer going to support cows, and we didn't want them to grow up into brush. The state forester told us that we could get the seedlings free and that in twelve years we would have fence posts. In twenty years we'd have lumber, a veritable gold mine.

47

George and I, the two girls, Patty's boyfriend, two forestry students, and George Turner, a forester, spent two unrelenting days tucking those spindly little pines into the ground. We did it under George Turner's supervision. The girls and I each had a pail of water filled with the baby pines. The boys and men dug a "V" with a pick-mattock (borrowed from Jimmy Pizzagalli's father's construction company). The female serfs dropped in a seedling, pressed the soil, and did an Indian dance around each transplant. One of the boys said wistfully, "Someday I'll bring my children and tell them that I planted that pine forest." He would now be fifty-eight and probably a grandfather.

Before they reached fence-post size all of the trees developed a disease and grew crooked. The new state forester said we should have planted red pine. Now they tell us! We had to have fifteen taken down some years ago at the cost of $1,500 because they were tangling with the phone and telephone wires. The trees crowded into so much shade around the house that we had to have the lights on all day. No one wants crooked trees for lumber.

So this year I hired six large men and two enormous trucks to come with chain saws and cut down twenty more trees. Sunlight poured into the house through suddenly dirty windows. I now have piles of logs in inaccessible places, brush that was dragged off into the woods, and $1,000 less in my checking account.

Forget the fence posts, the pine boards, and the historical mast for the king's navy. A neighbor who sells wood says he can't get his truck near enough to the logs. A chipper company would have to put in a road and then clear cut. That would have suited the early settlers of Vermont. They would build their cabins out of the boards and split the rest for heating and cooking. But I've become accustomed to creature comforts, and my back objects to sawing, splitting, and carrying wood in and ashes out.

Little did we know that our bargain of 1959 would become the most expensive fifteen acres of woodlot in the village of Jericho. We should have had a crystal ball to tell us that chipping companies can't maneuver their trucks on rocky hillsides, that wood-burning neighbors want logs piled near the driveway, and that your muscle power at eighty-three is not the same as it was at thirty-eight. Oh well, I'm enjoying the sunshine and the improved view of the brook.

May! Spring at Last!

May is my favorite month. Everything is fresh and new and full of the miracle of life. When we had animals it was always in May when we would get two baby pigs, chunky little six-week-olds charging around their pen like determined tugboats. Spring lambs were out on the newly green meadows, leaping straight up in the air and trying to get their sedate mothers to join in the fun. I love to visit the Morgan horse farm in May to see what one small grandson called "the horse puppies." Each snub-nosed leggy colt shadows his mare and then gallops off down the paddock at full speed, exulting in the excitement of being alive.

There's a burst of color in May. After the long dark winter, which sometimes seems monochromatic, there is an explosion of greens. The tiny waxy maple leaves are shining golden green. Fuzzy pale green ferns hunch up beneath the chartreuse cloud of poplar leaves. Dark green spears of onions and pale curls of lettuce are next to the pewter blue-green tendrils of peas. This is the month to plant the rest of the garden. Old-time Vermonters always waited until Memorial Day to put in the garden. But who can wait to get a head start with the cool-loving vegetables like spinach, peas, and lettuce? It will be a month before you're eating them, but you can always thin out the tiny lettuce leaves and pea-sized radishes to perk up your store-bought lettuce salads. And if you have an asparagus bed, you're now beginning to cut the first slender spears. If you don't have asparagus, find some fiddleheads curling up out of the ground in moist areas near rivers or brooks. Be sure to pick only the ostrich fern, the one with papery brown scales. The ferns with fuzzy, cream-colored fronds that you see along every roadside are not the ones you want to eat.

Unlike most people, I love dandelions. My idea of a beautiful landscape is a wide green meadow spangled with a thousand dandelions and a flock of ewes grazing with their lambs. At the edge of the meadow wild apple trees are bouquets of pink and white between the mists of pale green "popples."

A ride through the countryside in May is a kaleidoscope of chocolate brown new-plowed fields, bright green and gold meadows, clear blue skies, white farmhouses, and red barns. Why can't May go on forever? I would gladly exchange winter-weary March and somber November for two extra Mays.

The name May came from the Anglo-Saxon *Thrimilae,* meaning that you could milk your cows three times a day because they were gorging on the new grass. *Maia* was the goddess of growth, and the Dutch word *bloumaand* means blooming month. In the French revolution *floréal* was the time between April 20 and May 20.

The old song "Here We Go Gathering Nuts in May" wasn't about nuts at all. Nuts are gathered in November. It was "knots" of May, a nosegay of Mayflowers. Does anyone make May baskets anymore? It was a lovely old-fashioned custom. You hung a small basket of wildflowers on the doorknob of someone you admired, rang the bell or knocked on the door, and then ran to hide nearby before the honored one opened the door.

So go out in the woods and gather some violets, anemones, hepaticas, and maybe even a columbine and surprise someone who would be delighted to share your enjoyment of the extravaganza of May.

The Dark Ages?

"It must have been weird when you were young, grandma. That was before *everything*."

Different, yes, but not weird. We didn't know what we were missing. It's true that we lacked computers, television, credit cards, and Ben and Jerry's, without which my grandsons consider life an empty shell. We thought hardware was nuts and bolts. A chip was a small piece of wood, and we were taught in physics that nuclear fission was impossible. We thought fast food was something you ate during Lent. Smoking was cool. Grass was something you mowed with a hand mower on warm summer evenings, coke was a carbonated beverage, and pot was a cooking utensil. We didn't have electric typewriters or word processors. We didn't take a year off to "find ourselves" because we didn't know we were lost. Our closets were for putting clothes into, not for coming out of, and gay meant lighthearted and cheerful.

On the bright side we did *not* have AIDS, fear of atomic bombs, pierced navels, or carcinogenic food. If it was—carcinogenic, that is—we didn't know it. No male was allowed above the first floor in the girls' dormitory, and we hadn't heard of date rape.

What we did have was five-and-dime stores where you actually bought things for a nickel or a dime. Five cents bought you a bus ride, a phone call, an ice cream cone, or postage for two letters and a postcard. We wore girdles that had garters attached, and our dates wore suits. (That's when the jacket and trousers were made out of the same material.) Both sexes wore hats and gloves. A girl's pocketbook held no credit cards but had a compact and a fountain pen. An Ivy League college cost $500 for room and board and $500 for tuition per year. State universities cost much less. We mailed our laundry home in black cardboard laundry cases, and it came back clean with cookies and the local paper.

We had big bands: Guy Lombardo, Tommy Dorsey, and Glenn Miller. We had songs that you sang and danced to like "Body and Soul," "Smoke Gets in Your Eyes," "Night and Day," and "The Very Thought of You." We had romance. We thought that love was a precursor to sex and that a husband was a prerequisite for motherhood.

What we had was a lot of hope and enthusiasm and the belief that we would make the world a better place. Did we make it better? Perhaps yes, in technical ways, but not in terms of world peace and racial equality. Perhaps my grandsons won't either, but I will do whatever I can to encourage them to try.

Summer Soap Opera

I don't care how much wood my woodchuck would chuck if he could chuck wood. Because he wouldn't. He'd rather spend the winter dreaming about the succulent fare I will prepare for him in midsummer.

I live in a fool's paradise when I plant in mid-May and begin to enjoy the first radishes and lettuce a month later. Not until the blue-green tendrils of peas are about to blossom and the beans are in full leaf does the local wildlife take any interest in my garden. Then one day near the end of June I saunter down to admire my flourishing wide rows and POW! The peas have been eaten down to three-inch stems, the beans are defoliated, and the carrot tops have been shorn off as neatly as a crew cut. If you are a gardener, this trauma is right up there with Mt. St. Helen's and the Atlanta bomb. I don't know anything short of being robbed that is such a personal affront. Of course it *is* being robbed. The woodchuck could thrive just as well on all the lush vegetation outside my garden. If he could read I'd post it. Mrs. Appleyard was convinced her woodchuck did read and heeded her admonitions. Instead, I drag out the big Hav-a-hart trap—it's too heavy to carry, so I pull it down to the garden with a rope—set it, and hope that I'll find it occupied in the morning. The next morning the bait is gone and so is the woodchuck, but the trap has not been sprung.

I walk all around the fence looking for a likely hole under the fence or, better yet, a fresh woodchuck hole outside the fence. There are lots of weak places in the fence because it hasn't been repaired in years. A determined woodchuck could almost lean his way in. So each night I set the trap and each morning I find the bait gone and the trap empty. Some rat poison in the garage says "just one bite," so I think that while a woodchuck is considerably bigger than a rat, several bites might do him in. Wrong. He seems to love the taste of it, in fact, but at least he leaves my vegetables alone in favor of the poison.

One morning the empty trap is upside down, and the ground around it is all churned up as though there had been a struggle. He had been trapped but was able to release the bail and get out. But how long am I going to buy expensive rat poison to deter him from the vegetables?

So I buy a large square of that netting you put over a cherry tree or blueberry bush to discourage the birds. It doesn't cover the whole garden, but I put it over the beans, carrots, and parsley, hoping they will try to grow again. The parsley has not been touched so far. Maybe he doesn't like it. Wrong again. He chomps down the whole row right through the netting. Didn't the netting get caught in his teeth?

I take one more trip around the outside of the garden, which is very overgrown and bushy. At last I find a woodchuck hole and remember that I have a bomb from last year. I don't like setting those bombs. I did it last year out of desperation, but the warning notice says, "DANGER. You have five seconds between the time you light the fuse and the bomb explodes. Insert it as far as possible in the hole." Sure! It takes several seconds to light it and get it in the hole. You don't feel much like reaching in very far. So Bob Bechard, my goodhearted neighbor, offers to light it for me. I had prepared a pile of rocks and earth to jam over the hole after the bomb is lit. He lights the fuse, puts it in the hole, and just barely covers it when VOOM!—wisps of fumes creep out around the hole. We retire speedily, holding our breath.

Now I know a woodchuck has two entrances, but I can't find the other one and pray that he had been at home and asleep. I hope my troubles are over. Wrong again. A gardener's troubles are *never* over. Two days later the hole is open, and all of my squash plants have been eaten. Now would you prefer prickly squash leaves and stems to acres of red clover? I am now an authority on woodchuck preferences. They do not like tomatoes, peppers, asparagus, basil, or onions. They do like everything else, including all cucurbits, nasturtiums, chard, and all members of the cabbage family. I don't grow corn. Why should I do all that work for the raccoons? Raccoons have never come into my garden until the night before the corn is ready to be picked. Someone suggests a deer, but a deer can't reach into a Hav-a-hart trap and take out the bait. Maybe it's a woodchuck *and* a deer. Last year I put my granddog's hair, aluminum pans, soap, and wind chimes down there, but nothing worked until we successfully bombed the woodchuck hole.

My neighbors feel so sorry for me that they invite me to pick beans and peas from their gardens. I'm grateful, but I won't rest until the woodchuck gets what he deserves. Don't talk to me about cruelty to animals. What about animal cruelty to gardeners? And don't tell me to give up gardening. That is not an option. I could no more retire my hoe than I could stop breathing. In fact, my garden and the physical, emotional, and psychological benefits of it nourish me—my garden is what's keeping me breathing regularly at my advanced age.

Will I outlive the woodchuck? His life expectancy is shorter than mine is, but I have already used up most of mine. I'm determined to shorten his, and you are invited to his funeral if I am able to trap, poison, or shoot him. Well, maybe not shoot—how can I when I can't figure out how to pull the trigger with my fingers in both ears?

Video Venture

One morning John Bland phoned to ask if I would come over to his house to be on a video called "Life beyond 100!" Well, I'm not quite pushing 100 yet, but I've known John and Libets for nearly fifty years, and we qualify as octogenarians who are active and productive. He has received a lot of attention from the media recently because of his best-selling book *Live Long and Die Fast*. A research company in Florida was making a privately funded video on older people who lead active lives and medical research in the field of aging.

They needed a female token oldie, so I set out for Cambridge expecting fun. It was. It was more than fun. It was a comedy of errors with a happy ending.

On Pleasant Valley Road I passed an out-of-state car with two men in the front seat parked at the side of the road. It crossed my mind that they might be the photographer and the producer, confused by the Vermont back roads. For once, putting sense before sensibility, I decided to mind my own business and continued to the Blands.

"They should have been here an hour ago," John said, "God knows where they are now." So I told him about the two men I'd seen, and John set off to find them. Half-an-hour later John returned—no video men. Another thirty minutes passed. Finally, in drove the two guys I had seen by the side of the road. They had driven on to Cambridge for more directions and backtracked on Westman Road.

They set to work. John was to ride the horse to show them a bit of dressage, but the horse had gone off looking for greener pastures. Linda Bland offered to hunt for the horse. In the meantime, John was to get on the tractor and drive around looking capably rural. The tractor wouldn't start. A short delay followed while John, the photographer, and the producer crawled under and over the tractor. They emerged to suggest that they could interview me while waiting for the horse.

They set up a folding chair on the lawn and hung a microphone around my neck. I sat down, and the chair collapsed under me. The cameraman mercifully turned off the video while I scrambled back into an upright position.

I felt sorry for the two men, but they were having a fine time. They had been at research centers in California, Boston, North Carolina, and New Orleans, and they thought that this foray into the wilds of northern Vermont was a great adventure.

We departed in good humor, and two months later I received my copy of the video. It was two hours long, most of it scientific discourses on the causes of aging and what can be done about it. I appeared for one minute seated firmly in my wobbly chair, and there were several scenes of John driving the recalcitrant tractor and riding the horse, all very serene and bucolic.

But Dick Clark would have loved the out-takes.

Point of View

When I was a teenager I thought octogenarians were as strange as octopi. It was inconceivable that I would ever be *that* old. Now that I am one—octogenarian, not octopus—I'm beginning to think that teenagers may be the strange ones. They wear pants three sizes too big that fold and drag around their heels like mufflers. They poke holes in sensitive parts of their anatomy. Their speech is limited to "No way!" or "Right," and they use "like" and "y'know" in place of commas and periods. "We went downtown like cruising y'know and hung like all afternoon y'know" No, I don't know.

Girls favor black for prom dresses, either mid-thigh or floor length, but for every other occasion grunge is in. Boys own thirty-nine t-shirts (I counted my grandson's), twenty-five caps worn backwards and never removed, and five pairs of trail boots, casuals, and sneakers in various stages of disintegration.

I have to admit they aren't dirty. They just look that way. They shower at least once a day and spend a lot of time fussing with their hair. A boy may wear dreadlocks and a girl may spend all her allowance at a beauty parlor having her hair made to look snarled and wispy. The girls either wear no make up or purple lipstick and nail polish. They wear panties that are almost G-strings, but the boys now wear almost knee-length boxer shorts. Girls may wear granny boots, platform shoes, or stiletto heels.

They know how to ski and snowboard, ride mountain bikes, and surf the net, but they don't know a salad fork from a pitchfork. I'm not sure they know what a pitchfork is, either. They know how to set up a program for the computer, but they don't know how to spell the words. They don't need to. The computer will do it for them. They don't know how to write a thank you note or any reason why they should write one.

I have three grandsons. They are great, and not all of my remarks apply to them. They do thank me by telephone. I admire their technical skills, their athletic ability, their cavity-free teeth (thanks to fluoride), and their strong muscles. They are not nearly as tongue-tied as their peers, and they don't say "like" or "y'know" every other word, at least not to me. And their speech is not sprinkled with four letter words—again, at least not to me.

I can remember my grandmother being amused at my slang expressions and amazed at my floppy galoshes and yellow slicker, on the back of which I had painted a life-size illustration of a comic strip character. Do I look as weird to teenagers as they sometimes look to me? Of course I do. Who am I kidding? Would I want to be their age again? NO WAY! I don't want another ride on that roller coaster or the years of doubt and discovery. They may never have heard of Will Rogers, Caruso, ration books, or Marlene Dietrich, but for years I didn't know that The Who was a band or what teams were playing in the Super Bowl.

I know who I am now and am quite happy to be in my own skin. It could use pressing and spot remover, but it's my skin, and I'm attached to it.

A Place for Everything

"A place for everything and everything in its place" has an authoritative ring. It is essential for library books and cabinets, but it didn't always work for our rural menagerie

When we moved from New York City to a farm in Vermont, we had the space and the desire to have animals. Ninety acres, two empty barns, a horse stall, a chicken house, and another shelter we called the duck house simply called out for occupants. After all, why had we taken on a farm if we didn't plan to farm it?

I can't honestly say we were farmers because a farm in Vermont is supposed to have cows. George worked full time at the college, and I didn't want to milk cows twice a day and spread manure twice a year.

But, when George was asked how much we farmed, he always said, "As much as my wife's back can stand." My back was forty years younger. He rototilled the garden and built a pigpen and a raised turkey house in Jericho because, when we moved from South Burlington to Jericho each summer, we naturally brought everyone with us. When you take on animals it's till death do you part, even though we arranged their deaths. When the girls talked us into the horse or Debbie's dog, they vowed to take over the entire care, but somehow our horse and dog didn't measure up to the ones they had admired on TV.

It all sounds so simple. You just put the horse in the stall or pasture, house the chickens and ducks in their appropriate enclosures, and all you have to do is feed and water them twice a day. Ha! A six-week-old pig is about the size and shape of a bolster pillow and looks much too fat to squeeze through the two-inch spaces between the boards of the pigpen. Wrong! The spirit of Houdini lives on in piglets. One minute they're frolicking happily in the shavings in their pen, the next they're trotting in tandem across your unfenced hay field.

On one occasion my neighbors Pud and Ed Hill and I chased them all over the field, up the driveway, across Hinesburg Road, and into Rollin Tilley's driveway. Rollin, who had been enjoying our performance, threw a big net over all of us, immobilizing not only the two piglets, but also two forty-year-old farmers and one exhausted ex-urbanite—me.

In South Burlington we had a real chicken house with roosts and nests, and our hens stayed where we had unloaded them as ready-to-lay pullets. In Jericho George converted a horse stall into a chicken motel, using the mangers for nests.

The turkeys were a different matter. You can't house them with chickens or they—or the chickens—will develop Black Leg, a kind of avian Black Plague. So the turkey poults had to start out their life with us in the cellar of the South Burlington house in a raised cage next to the washing machine. They peep loudly, and it was interesting to see the looks on our dinner guests' faces when they heard strange noises that seemed to come from right under the dining-room table. It was even more interesting if you opened the cellar door and the strong ammonia fragrance wafted up the stairs.

But at least they didn't escape in South Burlington. When we moved them up to Jericho they were about chicken-sized, and George had built them a raised, covered cage behind the barn. They didn't get out of that either, but they had suicidal tendencies. Like sheep, turkeys are easily frightened. One time a low-flying plane buzzed our place, and the turkeys dashed to one corner, trampling each other. When the huddle untangled, two turkeys were dead.

In our experience, sheep rivaled turkeys for being beasts of little brain. They were always convinced that the grass just beyond the fence was tastier, and they would shove under or try to leap over the fence. Jackie Gleason, so named because he was born during the show of that name, was the appointed leader of our small flock. The others followed him like guess what. When he came out of the barn and a ray of sunlight was across the doorway, he jumped over it. So did the ewes. When he found that he could get over the fence in winter by climbing a snow bank, he kept trying in vain to vault the fence at that same spot long after the snow had melted.

The horse stayed in the stall most of the winter. So when she did get out in the spring, she galloped around wildly and refused to be caught, reducing me to oaths of frustration. Eventually the sound of oats rattling in a tin brought her close enough for me to grab her.

Over the years I chased pigs, sheep, a goat, and horses enough miles to qualify for the marathon. So now, at my advanced age, having been there and done that, I have no livestock, not even a dog, cat, or goldfish. I miss the murmuring of the hens and the fresh eggs. I miss the fun of watching the pigs, but I don't miss chasing animals through the underbrush, tackling a kicking sheep, or shoving an uncooperative pig into a station wagon.

Nothing is out of its place now, unless I have misplaced it. Would you care to hear how often that seems to happen? I didn't think so.

The Sound and Scent
of August

Shut your eyes and listen to August. Even without the other four senses you can recognize the season by the sounds. An August sound at my house is the click-clack of the baler on the hillside meadows across the brook. And down at the pool in the brook small boys are shouting as they leap off the rocks into the deep water below the waterfall. It is impossible for small children to be in the water without shrieking and screaming.

For four years, when we lived in Kansas, we only had one month, July, in Vermont. When we returned to Kansas we were greeted by a deafening chorus of cicadas.

If you were to paint August it might be a haying scene under threatening clouds, the whole family rushing to get the hay in the barn before the first big drops fall. You can almost hear the distant rumble of thunder. Swallows would be twittering under the eaves.

In my childhood lawn mowers were a dominant sound. Fathers mowed the lawns with hand mowers on summer evenings, while the mothers gathered in the sweet-smelling laundry from the line or sat on the porch, rocking and fanning themselves with palm-leaf fans. We played kick the can or one old cat in the largest lawn in the neighborhood.

In many Vermont villages there are weekly band concerts on the village green. The smallest children, some already in pajamas, march and leap around the bandstand in time to the music, dashing back now and then to the safe haven of their nearby parents. The concerts vary in the quality of the performance from town to town, but never in the quality of this quietly social time spent relaxing on blankets or in small family groups on folding chairs brought from home.

August has scents evocative of long ago summers— the delicate fragrance of wild roses on Martha's Vineyard, the smell of balsam woods on a hot summer day in South Bristol, Maine, the pungent odor of the tidal flats at low tide, part sea weed, part clams and minuscule marine life. The smell of wet pine logs takes me back to the Kennebec River when the logs were floated down the river to the pulp mills at Waterville. In my own fields there is the heavy sweet perfume of milkweed blossoms, and in the garden the distinctive sharp smell of the tomato vines clings to my hands and follows me up to the house until it dissipates in green suds.

August is a cornucopia of the senses—wood smoke, the sizzle and aroma of hamburgers on the grill, the contrast between the heat of noon and the soothing evening breeze under a peach-colored full moon.

The Distant Tinkle of Wedding Bells

I get an occasional letter or a phone call from someone who feels acquainted with me through my books. Only once have I received a hate letter, and that was from a man who felt I had portrayed him as eccentric. He was right, but so was I—he *was* eccentric. Nevertheless, I learned then that if you put someone in a book, you must do it with love or at least respect.

Eight years ago I had a phone call from an unknown and elderly lady in Ontario. I happened to be in the garden, quite a distance from the house. George was terminally ill at the time, but he dragged himself to the phone. The conversation went like this:

"I want to speak to Mrs. Wolf."

"I'm sorry, she's in the garden."

"Well, get her! I'm calling from Ontario. Go get her!"

The garden is within shouting distance from the house, but George wasn't strong enough to shout. He rang a cowbell, and I dashed to the house fearing an emergency.

That was the first of many calls from this lady, who had read a book of mine and felt that we must be soulmates. She's the one I wrote about in *Postmark Vermont* who told friends to find me during their trip to New England and take a picture of me and our brook. The only thing remarkable about that was that they arrived with a police escort. They had come as far as Essex, and, seeing a parked state trooper's car, they asked the trooper how to get to Nashville Road in Jericho.

He called the police dispatcher, who phoned me for directions. The trooper led them eight miles to my house, greatly impressing them with his cordial service. Having reached their destination at last, they snapped the pictures and took them to my phone pal in Ontario.

After that this ninety-year-old maiden lady phones me two or three times a year to talk about her Jersey calves and express the hope that sometime she will get down to see me.

Last fall she called again and announced, "My boyfriend and I are going to get married at your brook!" I was speechless. "He is 87 and I am 91, but I'm not very well. I don't get out."

When my voice came back I told her that the path down to the brook is very steep and rocky. "I doubt if you could make it," I ventured. "My athletic son-in-law fell on the path on his wedding day. Wouldn't you want to be married at home with friends and family?"

"No. I read about your daughter's wedding at the brook. I want to do that. Have you got any ministers in Vermont?"

"Yes, but I'm not sure they would think this was a good idea."

"Oh, and then we could all go out to dinner, minister too. You could arrange it."

Somewhat shaken and definitely troubled by this, I sat down and composed a long letter asking her to reconsider, that while we all like to dream about adventures like going to Tahiti or winning the lottery, they don't ever really happen.

A month elapsed and I was afraid I had hurt her feelings. Then she called again, chipper and as undeterred as ever.

"We've decided to wait till spring."

So much for my discouraging letter! I feel that I am living in a soap opera over which I have no control.

Stay tuned for the next episode.

The Last Days of Summer

It comes over me when I see a wash of goldenrod across the fields. Then one branch of leaves on a swamp maple turns scarlet. I look the other way and tell myself that that tree probably wasn't healthy—maybe it got too much salt from the road. But soon there are splashes of saffron on other trees.

The feeling of sadness cannot be denied. It marks the end of summer and the beginning of fall, our most spectacular season, bringing with it the inevitability of winter.

When the children were small, the brightening goldenrod reminded them that soon school would start, that they'd have to get up early in the morning and stagger out to the school bus. We tried to ameliorate this sense of impending doom by buying something new to wear to school on the first day—maybe a new lunch box, too—but the melancholy was pervasive at breakfast.

A friend who used to help me out in New York City always said, "It's never the job but the dread of it." How right she was! Once we tackle a distasteful chore or start the new school year, the foreboding dissolves and life shifts into a higher gear.

A neighbor of E. B. White called the last days of summer "suicide days." That seems a bit extreme, but Mr. White recognized and identified with the feeling that something ominous was hanging over him. The days may be perfect—warm, topped by blue skies tufted with snowy clouds—but they are too good to be true, too good to last.

When I taught school the last days of August were apt to be followed by nightmares of a traumatic first day of school—children crying, mothers upset, a child misplaced or injured—and I would wake with heart pounding and profound relief that it was only a dream. I haven't taught school for fifty years, and it is no longer my responsibility to pry small bodies out of bed and into stiff new clothes. But the September sadness drifts through the air with the thistledown and the milkweed seeds' silken parachutes. Goldfinches line their nests with thistle down. Imagine lying in a nest padded with gossamer filaments.

The portents of fall are all around us. I hear crickets chirp, and grasshoppers explode out of the grass as I walk down to the garden. The tomatoes are ripening too fast to eat but not enough to can. Besides, canning for one person seems like milking a mouse. That's what my kids used to call any job that seemed too big an effort for such a small return. Other chores in that category include prying nutmeats out of rock-hard black walnut shells, hulling tiny wild strawberries, and shelling fresh lima beans. I like the expression better than any of those jobs. Who would want to milk a mouse anyway?

The only cure for end-of-summer sadness is to plunge into the frenzy of harvesting. Dig the potatoes, pull up the onions, pick the early apples, and keep reminding yourself that you chose to live in a four-season (or five, if you count mud season) climate, so you must expect the transition from one season to the next. Each year you don't think spring will ever come, but it does. So you might as well enjoy the moment. The goldenrod is really very beautiful, the chicory is blue, the grass is growing at a much slower rate, and, best of all, the bugs have disappeared.

This burst of optimism is helpful but not curative. The sadness is still there, the realization that life is as short as a summer. There is an old Anglo-Saxon poem that describes life as a swallow that flies through the warmth and light of the great hall and then out into the dark again.

It is a flash in time, a momentary awareness of our mortality.

What's Good about Getting Older?

Before you answer "Not much!" let me point out several advantages besides the ten percent off at some restaurants, state parks, and drug stores. You don't have to show off anymore! Well, not "show off" exactly, but you don't have to dive into a pool when you are much more comfortable wading in, or go to a rock concert, or eat at a sushi bar when raw fish gives you a sense of impending doom.

And now you are mercifully free from those embarrassing moments when you were a teenager or young adult. They only seem funny now.

Recently, when I gave my seventeen-year-old grandson a ride to the dentist, I asked him if he was embarrassed to have me come with him. "No, because none of my friends are around here to see me with you." Fortunately, I can remember my own acute embarrassment as a teenager. My mother would speak up at a meeting or sing loudly in church. I wanted her to be seen and not heard, and preferably not even *seen* if her slip was showing or she was wearing sensible shoes.

One of my most humiliating adult moments was the posture picture taken during the first week of college, where you stood naked while some flunky dictated your statistics to someone in the gym department. There were no other spectators in the room, for which I was minimally grateful, but the litany of your anatomical abnormalities, shouted out loudly in the empty gym, took away what little self-esteem you had left. "Slight *lordosis*, right leg apparently longer than the left, poor posture, small breasts, pigeon-toed, florid skin." You bet it was florid! It is the only time in my life that I remember blushing.

Now, while I would not welcome a posture picture, I would be almost proud that at my advanced age I have held up as well as I have. The *lordosis*, unequal parts, and poor posture are still with me, but who cares when you are over eighty?

I think the difference is that in adolescence you are painfully self-centered. You are sure that everyone is looking at you, judging you, comparing you. Surprise kids! They're not. They're too busy thinking about themselves.

Another plus is that you don't have to win. When my grandsons were small they were obsessed with winning every indoor game. As five-year olds they would even cheat to get ahead. Winning was everything, and losing could precipitate a tantrum or the end of the game.

Winning means very little to me now. I like to be recognized and I like approval, but I don't have to win. In fact, it's nice just to be in the game. Not everyone feels that way. Dr. John Bland, runner and author of *Live Long, Die Fast*, enjoys the surprise of winning. It happens more frequently to him now because in his age group there are so few contestants that his chances of winning are greatly improved.

Think of all the worries that we have outgrown! Acne, pregnancy, AIDS, dating, jobhunting, climbing the corporate ladder. A medical student said to me, "You're lucky because all your problems are solved." True, I have outgrown *his* problems. I don't have to worry about getting an internship, getting married, establishing a practice, or repaying loans. I didn't tell him that there would always be problems. That is what life is, one challenge after another. He'll face them and solve them. But the lucky part about being old is that by now I've had a lifetime of experience in solving problems, and I know when and where to ask for help.

And now I can enjoy the four freedoms that come with age. Freedom from multiple family demands. Freedom from many household chores. Freedom to say "No." And freedom to be ME!

Actually, this is a pretty good time of life.

Gossamer Season

September is a gold rush. After the varietal greens of summer, nature's last green, like her first, is gold. Of course some summers aren't all that green—I remember one when lawns were brown and dry in July. None of us who live in the country and are dependent on our dug wells dared water the lawn or wash a car. Water was precious and only to be used for essentials. One neighbor of mine dipped out her bath water and carried it out to her flowers. Another lugged pails of water from her brook to keep her garden alive. Was it the drought that brought deer to our gardens in unusual numbers? My garden is fenced, but a four-foot fence is no deterrent to a deer.

Neither is a six-foot fence. I never saw my night visitor, but every morning it was depressing to see what had been cropped in the night. Their choice of snacks puzzled me. If you were a deer, would you have eaten rough pumpkin leaves and ignored tender lettuce? They enjoyed the snow peas and the sugar snap ones but left the big shelling peas alone. Carrot tops were mowed down to stubble.

I stopped in at a feed and garden store to ask for advice. Two men behind the counter and three shoppers heard the word "deer" and came over to add their tales of woe. All agreed that the best defense was a dog, but I don't really want the year-round care of a dog again. Debbie gave me a bag of dog hair each time she brushed her dog. That seemed to help for a while—until it rained, anyway. The man at the store suggested dried blood, and I scattered that around their favorite vegetables. Mothballs are supposed to be effective but dangerous for pets or children. Now that I have neither, I ringed the garden with moth flakes. Someone else said that rubbing soap on the fence was a deterrent, but that it should be Irish Spring! I tried Camay—no luck. It was a hard summer for gardeners.

But now in September we are in the season of gossamer and gold. The big purple thistles wear tufts of filaments that float through the air. Goldfinches pull them apart to eat the tiny seeds. Milkweed pods burst open, and clouds of milkweed fluff ride the breeze.

Gold is everywhere—goldenrod, goldfinches dipping over the meadow, sunflower heads following the sun, corn, and pumpkins. Even the unpicked cucumbers are fat, golden blimps hiding under their foliage.

It is a time of ripeness. The early apples and grapes perfume the air. Tomatoes are at their best, and we hurry to harvest them before the first frost. September has another gold: the big school buses that rumble up the roads filled with their shrieking cargo.

Nights are chilly and clear. If your neck can stand the strain, watch for meteors. If you don't see any falling stars, at least you will see a wonderful stellar display that seems brighter than in mid-summer.

There is a hint of the colder nights to come, but in the early morning a light blanket of fog lies over the lake and the river valleys. The sun lights up this gentle coverlet of mist with the pastel colors of opal, pale pink, aqua, and lemon before the warm sun burns off the fog.

September is bittersweet. The first frost is a harsh reminder that summer is over and that, after the conflagration of October, we must shore up and store up for the onset of winter.

Enjoy this mellow encore of blue and gold days when the sun is a warm presence on your back as you gather in the harvest of your golden garden.

Moose Watch

"I never saw a purple cow
I never hope to see one
But I can tell you anyhow
I'd rather see than be one!"

Until recently a moose on Nashville Road was almost as rare as a purple cow. I had only seen one in the forty-eight years we've lived here. Although our road is not paved, there are more than a hundred houses beyond mine, a condominium complex, and a golf club, all of which account for a steady stream of cars. It's not what I would call moose habitat. My house is on a rocky ledge high above a swift running brook but there is no swamp or marshy area conducive to the aquatic plants favored by moose.

So I did a double-take one day when I looked out the window to see a large female moose standing ten feet away. "There's a moose," I thought to myself and then shouted "It's a MOOSE!" She was equally surprised to see me, and we stared at each other stupidly. Something moved in the trees behind her—there was another moose, a female, somewhat smaller. But when I stepped out onto the porch close enough to touch them, they turned and loped away into the woods, their long thin legs moving with surprising speed.

I was so excited that I had to call my son-in-law, Steve Page in Williston, whose reaction was, "Now Maggie, are you sure it was a moose?" Come on, Steve, a moose at arm's length looks like nothing else. It may not be a thing of beauty, but it is impressive.

My nearest neighbors—Jenny and Richard, half a mile in one direction, and Claudia Bechard, three quarters of a mile down the road in the other direction—had not seen them, but they shared my excitement.

A few days later John Hart, a former teacher in South Burlington, drove into my yard. "Seen the moose?" He had seen them farther up the road toward Bolton Mountain.

When I stopped in to see Dianne Schullenberger's art exhibit one mile east and told her about my moose, she was not surprised. "One comes here quite often down by the pond, but a whole moose family really stopped traffic the other day."

A huge bull moose, a cow, and a calf were at the side of the road. The bull moose stepped out into the middle of the road, apparently expecting the cow and calf to follow him across. They didn't, so he just stood there. One car stopped, then another car, and then a school bus full of noisy children. The moose held his ground, effectively halting traffic in both directions. No one seemed eager to get out and shoo him away. Finally the cow and calf got the message and joined him in the middle of the road, whereupon he slowly led them across the road into the woods. The children in the school bus were enchanted. It's not every day that you arrive late to school with the excuse that a moose family held up the bus.

I had almost forgotten my moose visit when Bradley Westie met me on the village green and said she heard I had a moose in my yard and wanted to tell me about *her* moose. It seems that Bradley had been hankering for a pool and begged John to fix her something to immerse herself in on a hot day, even if it was a make-shift tub, hidden in the deep woods behind their house. John came through with a bath tub, spring-fed and secluded. One hot day Bradley escaped to her oasis, took off her clothes, sank into the cool depths up to her ears, closed her eyes, and luxuriated in her sylvan nook. When she opened her eyes, she looked right into the huge face of a full-grown moose.

Her first thought was, "What will the moose think? I haven't a stitch on!" Her second thought was that she wanted her boys to see the moose. She slowly stepped out of the tub, wrapped a towel around her, and ran back to the house, calling the boys. The moose was retreating by the time they came back, but at least he was visible, saving her from the disbelief of teen-age sons.

These moose sightings on our road haven't received the publicity of two other Vermont moose. Surely you remember the furor over the heifer Jessica and her Shrewsbury moose admirer, Bullwinkle. They attracted national media attention and quite a profit for Jessica's owner Larry Carrara. A true Yankee, never "loath to turn a penny in the way of trade," he was selling tee-shirts and welcoming the publication of a book about this unusual romance. All the world loves a lover, no matter how mismatched.

In February 1997, with Jessica and Bullwinkle only a memory, the small town of South Lincoln (the one that usually reports the coldest temperature and the heaviest snowfall in central Vermont) came into the spotlight. A young female moose moved into town and took up residence in a field near the road, oblivious to the stares of increasingly numerous moose watchers. The day I saw her she was standing in a driveway calmly returning the stares of her admirers, who were inching closer and closer to her. The children wanted to pat her enormous nose, which she placidly endured, but her self-appointed guardian advised them not to touch her body. She looked very fit. Her shiny, almost black coat glistened in the sunlight and her large brown head and long grey-brown legs showed no traces of trauma or illness. I was standing a foot away from her, the closest I have ever been to a moose, but I was somehow saddened by her passivity. I wanted her to snort and run away.

Was she near-sighted, slow-witted, or, like the fauna on the Galapagos, unaware that man is the enemy? Michael O'Keefe is now known in Island Pond as the "moose magnet," because he has the dubious distinction of having hit two moose in one day. He was not happy about it. Neither were the moose. Are we encroaching on their territory? The preservation of these handsome animals, as well as the preservation of our life, may well be in wildness.

October's Bright
Blue Weather

What is so rare as a day in June? A day in the first week of October. When I was in fourth grade, I had to memorize a poem which ended, "on the top of a hill, where all could see, God planted a scarlet maple tree."

When I drive through the golden tree tunnels and look out upon the conflagration of foliage on a crystal-clear October day, I recall that poem and my childhood pleasure in collecting scarlet and saffron maple leaves on my meandering walk home from school. I think children who ride the noisy yellow school buses miss the companionship and relaxation we enjoyed on those long walks, especially in October, with the smell of burning leaves and the excitement of finding horse chestnuts, shiny and satin-smooth to the touch.

October is a time of putting the garden to bed. Of course by then, unless we're unusually lucky, we've had a killing frost and much in the garden is limp and brown. But the beets and carrots are still in good shape. Brussels sprouts and kale are better after a few frosts. I notice that kale is becoming chic again and turning up in soups of European origin. You've brought in pumpkins and squash. Did you remember to cut a child's initials on a pumpkin when it was softball size so that now the name shows clearly on the side of that huge orange globe? Most local stores will be glad to pay you for your surplus. One year I made a deal with my young grandson. If he would help me cut and carry the pumpkins to the car, he could split the proceeds from our village store. Bonanza!

If you were wise enough to bring in your cutting flowers before the frost, you may still have several bouquets in the house. Zinnias brighten up a room with their peach, crimson, pale yellow, and apricot hues, many of the same colors of the autumn leaves that are drifting down outside, laying an oriental carpet under the trees.

Chrysanthemums are in full glory. Their spicy fragrance evokes October's bright blue weather. A walk along a country road is a great way to enjoy our wild gardens if you can pull your eyes down from the brilliant canopy overhead. Asters are everywhere, both the deep purple and pale lavender ones. Goldenrod plumes are turning silver among the wiry black-eyed Susans, and the torches of staghorn sumac turn wine red before the leaves burst into flame. The air is crisp and cool, but there is still warmth in the sun. If you prefer to ride through the countryside, stop now and then to store up images of the brilliant multi-colored hillsides to recall on a snowy winter day.

One of my favorite autumn scenes is the first snowfall dusting the top of Mount Mansfield. The hills are alive with color, but the top of the mountain is pure white against a morning glory blue sky.

Why can't October last? There is something sad in the soft sound of falling leaves and the cold nights that portend the coming of winter. The only antidote is to enjoy this beauty while it lasts. Picking apples is an October pleasure.

Joan and Jim Madison invite me to come to pick some of their beautiful apples on an October day when they are making cider. As you fill your canvas sack with the big fragrant Macs, the trees seem to be relieved of their heavy burden and spring back from your gentle twist. A few bees and hornets buzz around some fallen fruit, and the air is sweet with the scent of ripeness. I loved June, but isn't October equally rare?

What's in a Name?

More precisely, what's in *my* name? I am, and it
tells more about me than my social security number.
Like Caesar's Gaul it is divided in three parts: the name
given to me at birth, my father's name, and the name of
man I married. The world is full of Maggies—or Toms,
Dicks, and Harrys—but I've never known a Maggie who
had all three of my names.

Henry Clark of Underhill sent me a wonderful article called "Don't Call Me Henry." He didn't write it.
It was written by Henry Catto, a former American am-
bassador to Great Britain. But it's not just his diplo-
matic background that makes him object to the infor-
mality of being addressed by his first name by people
he has never met. It's his age. Most of us who have passed
three score find it offensive when a gum-chewing re-

ceptionist in a bank or a doctor's office calls us by our first names at our first encounter.

When growing up we were expected to call anyone older by the title of Mr., Mrs., or Miss. It would have been as rude to call my mother's friend "Sarah" as to ask her age. We called her "Aunt Sarah," which meant that she was a close friend, almost a relative. Now I'm not advocating a return to white gloves and calling cards, but sometimes, like Rodney Dangerfield, I would like more respect. I've gone to the same hair stylist for twenty-five years. We have shared a lot of family experiences, and I feel we are friends, but she still calls me Mrs. Wolf and that enhances her dignity as well as mine.

Too often a doctor calls a patient by her first name, but can you picture the surprise on his face if she called him "Tom"? He puts on the dignity of his profession along with his white coat. True I call my internist by his first name, but I have known him since he was a medical student. I asked if that offends him, and he said, "Not if it is a friend, but if a patient calls him by his first name in a condescending way, he feels demeaned." That's what I'm talking about. No one likes to be patted on the head at any age.

My daughter's friends are introduced only by first names. I often discover later that I know one of their parents, and it would have been nice to make that connection when meeting them.

I don't expect the waiter in a restaurant to tell me his whole name. In fact, I don't see any reason for him to tell me his first name or to turn up every few minutes to check on my welfare. If I need him I can get his attention without calling out "Michael" or "Robert."

My husband played squash every day with Dr. Harold Wolff (no relation) at New York Hospital. Dr. Wolff always called George "Dr. Wolf," and George never dreamed of calling his revered mentor "Harold." They had great respect for each other. My sons-in-law call me "Maggie," but I'm "Grandma" to my grandsons. They would be uncomfortable calling me "Maggie." The age span is too great for such a leap of intimacy.

What's in a name? "That which we call a rose by any other name would smell as sweet." I'm no rose, but I noticed that every rose in the Montreal botanical garden has its own name in both English and Latin.

What's Good about November?

November is not my favorite month. In fact, you can flip the leaf of your calendar right over—I won't mind. And while you're rearranging the calendar, why not take out March too and make spring come a little sooner? I don't complain much about Vermont weather, but taking out November and March would shorten the winter, still leaving December, January, and February for the skiers and lengthening our brief spring and fall by substituting an extra May and October. Wouldn't that be great, extending the vibrant fall foliage and welcoming the snowdrops, crocuses, and shadbush a month earlier?

But back to reality. The weatherman says that November is our greyest month, with only 30 percent of possible sunshine. Everywhere you look nature's last gold has turned to silver. Well, not everywhere. The tamaracks thrust up golden candles among the dark evergreens, but the goldenrod's fire has turned to ash. Streams look like molten lead under grey skies, and the once green fields are now muted shades of grey and brown.

It is a time of tidying up the garden. Deep within us is some atavistic urge to gather and store up the fruits of our summer labors. It used to be called putting food by and was a time to admire the glass jars of jellies, pickles, and canned fruits and vegetables. Many of those are frozen now, but I still like to count the pickles and jellies. The satisfaction of working in tandem with nature to provide food to carry us through the winter is a November pleasure even though every roadside stand and supermarket is bursting with similar produce.

In his article in the beautiful book *Vermont for Every Season,* John Vachon calls November "Days of Grace." It is a time after the exuberance of October and before the onset of winter, when seasonal growth is over and we look inward rather than out. On a cold November day the contrast between the sharp nip of frost outdoors and the warmth of an open fire is appreciated for the first time in the season.

High in the sky "V" formations of geese fly south, the haunting sound variously described as sleigh bells or the baying of "the hounds of heaven." We watch them fade into the distance in awe, knowing that winter is on the way. The first real snowfall comes in November to the delight of the hunters and early skiers. I am neither, but I do admit that the bare brown fields are more attractive dressed in white.

Thanksgiving gives a country person a showcase for his produce. When we had pigs, chickens, and turkeys we took pride in growing almost everything on the Thanksgiving table. One of our own turkeys was stuffed with our own sausage, onions, and parsley. The squash, pumpkins, potatoes, and apples were home grown. Even the lard in the pie crust came from our pigs, but who would admit to using lard these days?

There are other things to be thankful for. By dinner time on Thanksgiving the football season is over, and every mother of teen-age and college-age sons breathes a sigh of relief that her son has only minor bruises to show for the time he spent on the bottom of the heap.

I am always thankful when hunting season is over. For two weeks the woods are alive with hunters in camouflage or red and orange clothing. On every back road three or four of them lean against ancient cars, a beer can in one hand and a gun in the other. Bonding and drinking clubs locally known as deer camps lure the male population from the TV football games, and wives and mothers are thankful when the weary and bleary hunters return, perhaps unsuccessful but unscathed.

There is nothing lovelier than a doe with twin fauns or a proud buck standing on a hilltop, but I can't help being thankful that the herd has been reduced. In spite of every deterrent I have tried the deer eat more of my garden than I do. And I no longer wince when I hear shots in my woods.

November leaves me cold, figuratively and literally. Maybe I was meant to be a hibernating animal. But before I dig in for the winter I am thankful that Thanksgiving is over and a blanket of snow insulates the land. Now I'll take a deep breath and look forward to Christmas.

The Star of Bethlehem

And here it is Christmas again! When you are very small the long wait for Christmas seems to last forever. When you get to be a grandparent the season is upon you before you have finished the Thanksgiving turkey soup.

It shouldn't come as a surprise. The stores and catalogues have been flaunting Christmas since Hallowe'en. We knock ourselves out in an effort to celebrate the season when what we really want for Xmas is as simple as "my two front teeth," something that shows that the giver cares about you.

What do you remember about Dickens' *Christmas Carol*? It's not Scrooge or Marley's ghost—it's the warmth of the Cratchet family, the small voice of Tiny Tim saying "God bless us everyone," the ray of hope, the promise that the birth of Christ could change the world. In the midst of the commercialism, the gaudy displays, the crowded stores, and the surfeit of things to buy, the spirit of Tiny Tim is in every "Merry Xmas!" It is in the man who smiles as he holds the door for you, the excitement of the child wrapping up presents in secrecy, the search for the one gift that will show that the giver was thinking of you in a special way.

Although I admit I have succumbed to sending gift certificates with the excuse that I don't know what the person needs or wants, the real fun in Christmas is when you find or make the exact right present. There is always the urge to spend more than you planned or make something that takes a lot of time and patience. It is the desire to give. And isn't that what the birth of Christ was about? In spite of the hoopla, the hype, and the catalogues, Christmas is about the gift of love.

When my father was a boy, a homemade toy and an orange in his stocking were rare treats, tokens of sacrifice and love. We all want everyone to be happy—unrealistic though that is at times—but it isn't achieved by buying the most expensive gift or the latest electronic device. It comes from showing that you care. It can be a phone call, a box of cookies, a load of manure, or a cord of wood. The fun is in the planning.

Do you remember the excitement of waking on Xmas morning and knowing that it really *was* Xmas? Of course you looked forward to exploring the knobby contents of your stocking and unwrapping the mysterious gifts under the tree. But you also waited in suspense as your mother unwrapped the bookmark you had stenciled with her initials. Only half of Christmas is receiving presents. The other half is giving a bit of yourself with each gift. The birth of Jesus was a gift of love.

The greatest gifts we can give our children are warm family traditions that represent the true spirit of Christmas. Peace on earth, goodwill toward men.